WRITING VIVID EMOTIONS:
Professional Techniques For Fiction Authors

by Rayne Hall

Writing Vivid Emotions: Professional Techniques For Fiction Authors

by Rayne Hall

Book cover by Erica Syverson and Uros Jovanovic

© 2017 Rayne Hall

January 2017 Edition

ISBN-13: 978-1542578028

ISBN-10: 1542578027

All rights reserved. Do not reproduce this work in whole or in part without Rayne Hall's written permission.

British English.

CONTENTS

INTRODUCTION 5

CHAPTER 1:
HOW TO CONVEY EMOTION THROUGH
BODY LANGUAGE 7

CHAPTER 2:
VISCERAL REACTIONS..12

CHAPTER 3:
DIALOGUE..15

CHAPTER 4:
TONE OF VOICE..17

CHAPTER 5:
THOUGHTS 20

CHAPTER 6:
DESCRIPTIONS CONVEY MOOD..23

CHAPTER 7:
SIMILES 27

CHAPTER 8:
SECRET, SUPPRESSED AND FAKED FEELINGS 30

CHAPTER 9:
VARYING THE EMOTIONAL INTENSITY............................36

CHAPTER 10:
LAYERING EMOTIONS 38

CHAPTER 11:
STIRRING READER EMOTIONS 41

CHAPTER 12:
THESAURUS OF BODY LANGUAGE CUES 46

CHAPTER 13:
THESAURUS OF VISCERAL RESPONSES 55

CHAPTER 14:
TWO SAMPLE STORIES 63

DEAR READER, ... 76

ACKNOWLEDGEMENTS 77

EXCERPT:
WRITING DEEP POINT OF VIEW 78

INTRODUCTION

Do you want your characters to feel such strong emotions that the readers' scalps prickle, their mouths go dry and their hearts thud like they're sharing the experience?

Do you want to convey fear or happiness in ways that make the readers feel heat radiating through their chest or cold sweat trickling down their spine? This will pull them deeper into the story than than the tired 'he was afraid' or 'she felt happy'?

This book shows you professional techniques for creating and conveying emotions.

It covers three groups of feelings:

1. Emotions felt by the point of view (PoV) character, the one through whom the reader experiences the story or the scene.
2. Emotions felt by other characters whom the PoV character observes.
3. The readers' emotions as they read the story.

Each requires a different approach, and I'll show you the best way to handle them.

Step by step, you'll learn how to express feelings through body language, dialogue, thought, similes, visceral sensations and mood-rich descriptions. The book also guides you through layering emotions and varying their intensity. It shows you how to subtly reveal a character's secret or suppressed emotions.

The book also flags mistakes to avoid and reveals tricks used by professional authors. At the end of each chapter, you'll find assignments. If you like, you can use this book as an advanced fiction-writing course.

Each section gets directly to the point, making this a concise manual for writers who know what they want to achieve. This book is not suitable for absolute beginners. It assumes that you have mastered the basics of your craft and know how to create characters and write dialogue. If you're new to crafting fiction, I suggest you set this guide aside for now and start with a basic fiction-writing book.

To avoid clunky constructions like 'he or she did this to him or her', I apply sometimes the female pronoun, sometimes the male. Everything in this book applies to women and men equally. Please note: I use British English words, spelling, grammar and punctuation.

Now let's bring your characters' emotions to life.

Enjoy!

Rayne Hall

CHAPTER 1:
HOW TO CONVEY EMOTION THROUGH BODY LANGUAGE

When we feel an emotion, our bodies react. Our posture, facial expression, gestures, movement pattern, skin colour and tone of voice change, often without us being aware.

As writers, we can use body language to 'show don't tell' what a character feels.

Look at these examples:

He banged a fist on the table.
She slammed the door behind her.

As a reader, you don't need to be told that these characters are angry, do you? Their body language says it clearly.

These body language cues are much more effective than bland statements like:

He was angry.
She felt anger.

Body language is the number one tool for conveying character emotions. Psychologists refer to body language cues as 'tells' which is confusing for writers, since we use them to 'show don't tell'. That's why I prefer the word 'cue'.

BODY LANGUAGE IN DIALOGUE SCENES

Body language works great in dialogue. Put the body language cue in the same paragraph as what the character says, either before or after or in the middle. Then you can skip the dialogue tags (*'he said'*, *'she exclaimed'*), and you certainly won't need adverbs (*'he said angrily'*).

Here are examples of how you can handle the body language as a dialogue attribution beat with jaw-rubbing as the cue. People rub their jaws when they are uncertain about something but consider it favourably. These three variations show the beat placed after, before and in the middle of the spoken line.

"I suppose it's possible." John rubbed his jaw.
John rubbed his jaw. "I suppose it's possible."
"I suppose it's possible." John rubbed his jaw. "If you give the order, we'll try."

Body language can emphasise what the speaker says.

Mary glanced at her watch. "Hurry up. The train will leave in four minutes."
John's face brightened. "I'd love that."

CAUTION: DON'T USE BODY LANGUAGE THE POV CAN'T SEE

Who is the PoV character of this scene? If you show the experience from a specific character's perspective, you need to stay inside that character. Most of the time, people are unaware of their own body language, and they can't see their own facial expressions.

This means you can show only those bits of body language the PoV character is aware of or is doing deliberately - or those she observes in others.

If Mary is the PoV character, don't write

Mary's face grew pale.
or
A deep frown appeared on Mary's forehead.

because she simply can't see this.

Although you can use some forms of deliberate body language (*Mary slammed the door behind her*), it's best not to rely on body language for the PoV. In Chapter 2, I'll show you a better technique for conveying what the PoV feels.

OVERUSED NOVICE BODY LANGUAGE

When new writers discover body language, they often use the same narrow range of cues:

- smile
- frown
- shrug
- nod
- raise brow
- bite lip
- clench fist
- single tear

These are not wrong, but they get boring with repetition. Aim for more variety.

At the end of this book, I've compiled a Thesaurus of Body Language Cues where you can look up the emotions you want to convey and find several body language suggestions for each.

PROFESSIONAL TIP

To create tension, you can use body language that expresses the opposite emotion from what the character says, perhaps because she has to hide her true feelings.

"Take your time. I'm happy to stay a bit longer." Mary glanced at her watch.

"Yes, Sir." Mary's fingers clenched around the staff so tightly that her knuckles stood out white. "It will be my pleasure."

ASSIGNMENTS

1. Take the scene you're currently working on. For each character - other than the PoV - identify one emotion. Choose a way to express this with a body language clue. The Thesaurus of Body Language Cues in Chapter 12 has suggestions you can use.

Write a body language sentence for each of the characters, and insert it into the scene, perhaps as a dialogue attribution beat.

2. Observe the body language of strangers. Watch someone - their posture, their gestures, their facial expressions - and conclude how they feel. Write your observations down. Next time you want to show a character with those emotions, you have a ready-made description.

You may want to repeat this exercise whenever you're in a place with several people and have the leisure to take notes. For example, in the dentist's waiting room you may see a woman who clutches her bag close to her chest, frequently shifts in her seat, touches her throat and bites her lips. She's clearly afraid of the dentist. The man next to her keeps tapping his foot, glancing at his watch and frowning at the door of the consulting room. Obviously he's impatient and annoyed that he hasn't been called yet.

You can do your people-watching in railway stations, bus stops, supermarket aisles, laundrettes, coffee shops, pubs, bowling alleys, playgrounds, wherever there are people. Do you have to attend pointless, drawn-out meetings? Use the time constructively by studying body language, gathering cues for eagerness, boredom, and irritation.

Observe, analyse, memorise and keep notes. Just be discreet, and don't stare obviously at anyone. Your subjects must not notice that they're being watched.

If you can't leave the house or feel self-conscious watching people, watch a movie instead. Actors are trained to express emotion in body language, so watching their postures, gestures and facial expressions can yield a wealth of concise cues.

Rayne Hall

Before long, you'll have built an Emotion Descriptions Bank to drawn on.

CHAPTER 2:
VISCERAL REACTIONS

Instead of stating the emotion *(He was angry. She felt desire.)* describe its effects on the body. Every emotion brings physical symptoms. Sometimes we're consciously aware of them, for example, when gross injustice makes us nauseous or the supervisor's constant meddling causes us a painful stiffness at the back of our neck. These physical reactions are so common that they have given rise to the phrases 'this makes me sick' and 'a pain in the neck'.

These visceral reactions serve to convey what the PoV character feels. Where in the body does she feel it? How does it feel? Is the sensation hot or cold, pleasant or painful, expanding or tight? Does it itch, throb, churn or tingle?

Write a sentence about it. You can include the name of the emotion if you wish, although this is often not necessary.

If a fiction character is angry, a novice might write *'he felt angry'* which is bland and leaves the reader untouched.

Now consider an angry person's visceral reactions: churning stomach, acid feeling in the guts, tightness in the diaphragm area, quivering muscles in the upper arms, stiff neck, heat flushing through the body.

You might use these to write one of these sentences:

His stomach churned.
His neck stiffened.
Acid anger rose like undigested food from his stomach.
His biceps quivered, ready for a fight.
Heat washed through him in an angry wave.
He tried to rub the stiffness from his neck.

Let's take another emotion: desire. When a character desires someone or something, the physical symptoms include awareness of one's own heartbeat, warmth flooding the body, increased saliva in the mouth, tingling all over or just in the hands, fingers aching with the need to touch the person or object, faster breath, a pang in the heart area, a pleasant shiver all over or just in the upper body. (Erotic desire brings an additional set of reactions which I won't describe here.)

You might write sentences like these:

Her breath came faster, and her heart danced.
Warmth filled her chest, her heart, her mind.
Her fingers tingled.
Her palms burned with the need to touch his skin.
A pang in her chest released waves of yearning.

To find the right 'symptoms' of an emotion, draw on your own experience. How does desire feel to you? Where in the body have you felt anger?

At the end of this book, I have compiled a thesaurus of visceral reactions where you can look up the emotion and find relevant symptoms.

PROFESSIONAL TIP

To emphasise an emotion, cluster several symptoms. You can sprinkle them across several paragraphs or combine two in a single sentence like this:

Her heart pounded and her mouth went dry. (Fear)
His throat scratched and his vision blurred. (Sadness)

However, it's best not to put more than two visceral responses into one sentence.

WHAT NOT TO DO

Don't apply visceral reactions with a heavy brush. If you overuse them with a symptom in every paragraph of your story, your writing will feel heavy and the readers may find it tedious.

Instead, cluster several visceral responses when you want to emphasise emotions, and keep other sections visceral-free.

ASSIGNMENTS

1. Choose a situation in your work in progress (WiP) where the PoV character experiences an intense emotion: disappointment, jealousy, happiness, whatever.

Think of a time when you felt disappointed, jealous, happy. Conjure up the memory in detail. After a while, your mind will produce the physical symptoms. Write them down. Then tweak them to suit the character and situation, and insert a sentence or several into the scene.

You can supplement your memory with suggestions from the Thesaurus of Visceral Reactions Chapter 13.

2. Next time you experience an emotion - frustration, anger, desire, relief, boredom - observe the physical symptoms in your own body and write them down. You can do this in your journal, or directly into a structured file on your computer you can access easily. If you do this every time, you'll soon have a personal Emotion Descriptions Bank to draw on.

Venting troublesome emotions such as hurt, frustration and resentment on paper can be therapeutic. It's also a constructive use of your time when you're obliged to attend pointless meetings and presentations where the speaker goes on and on. Take your notebook and describe your symptoms of boredom - drowsiness, wandering attention, the need to clench your jaw to prevent a yawn. If you do this, others will think you're an attentive, note-taking listener, never guessing that you are working on a creative writing project.

CHAPTER 3: DIALOGUE

One of the easiest ways to show what characters feel is to let them talk.

"Hurry up." (Impatience)
"Stop picking your nose." (Irritation)
"Thank God." (Relief)
"What's this?" (Curiosity)
"Is that all we got?" (Disappointment)

Feelings affect the rhythm of how the characters talk. For example, a character who is impatient, frustrated or angry will use very short sentences, often phrased as commands or questions:

"Shut up."
"Snap out of it."
"How much longer?"
"Do we have to do this?"

Word choices convey the mood, too. A character who is pleased, happy or awed will refer to a mature woman as *'that old lady'*, a cat as *'the kitty'* and the rented room as *'her bedsit'* - but if he's annoyed, frustrated or resentful he may talk about *'that hag'*, *'the beast'* and *'her dump'*.

Swearwords can indicate anger, dislike and frustration, but use them sparingly, because they can put readers off and make characters appear unintelligent, which may not be the effect you want.

A character who feels uncertain or confused may intersperse his speech with phrases like *'maybe'*, *'kind of'*, *'in a way'*.

Dialogue tags can further clarify the mood. How does the character talk? Instead of *'she said'* you can write *'she snapped'*, *'she muttered'*, *'she grumbled'*, *'she croaked'*.

WHAT NOT TO DO

- Don't use a lot of swearwords, because they can make the speaker appear unintelligent, which may not be the effect you want.
- Don't use swearwords at all unless you're certain that your intended readership won't mind.
- Don't rely on dialogue as the main vehicle for emotions. Mix it with other techniques to give your writing emotional depth.
- Don't overdo the dialogue tags. Fewer is often better.
- Don't attach adverbs to dialogue tags. *('She said angrily.' 'He asked hopefully.')*
- Don't let characters explain their feelings. People rarely do that outside a therapy session.

PROFESSIONAL TIP

Mix the techniques discussed in this chapter with either body language or visceral responses. The combination creates vivid impressions and is a pleasure to read. It also means you won't need any dialogue tags, because the speaker is implied.

Examples:

Mary shrank away from him. "Don't hurt me. Please! I'll do anything you want."
My stomach soured. "Is this your idea of playing fair?"

ASSIGNMENT

Find a dialogue scene you've written. Identify what each speaker feels. Tweak what they say so their word choices and speech rhythms reflect their mood.

If you like, insert a few (but not many) expressive dialogue tags, and add body language cues for the non-PoV characters.

CHAPTER 4:
TONE OF VOICE

How does the character's voice sound when she talks? Describe it creatively.

Here are several methods. Although highly effective, they are best used sparingly, because they can become tedious if overused.

1. Use a dialogue tag that implies the sound. Instead of *'she said'* write *'she whined', 'she hissed', 'she shrilled', 'she croaked'*.

2. Describe the voice with a simile (a comparison):

His voice sounded as if ...
Her voice sounded like a ...

For a more vivid version, include a vivid verb:

His voice grated like a...
Her voice shrilled like a....

Place this description after the character has said something, or in the middle of the speech, but not before.

Here are two examples how you might use this method:

"I know we don't have the resources, but we have to make this work somehow." John's voice rumbled like a lorry up a country lane.

"We have to work overtime again, whether we want to or not." Mary's voice whined like an out-of-tune church organ. "Someone should tell them that this isn't fair."

With this method, you can leave out dialogue tags.

Instead of

"This is so sweet of you," Mary said. Her voice tinkled like bell.

You can simply write

"This is so sweet of you." Mary's voice tinkled like a bell.

Writing Vivid Emotions

This makes the writing tighter, faster-paced and more exciting.

Describing the tone of the speaker's voice works best for characters who are not the PoV. Use this method for the PoV if he is aware of how his voice sounds, for example:

"They were fine when I saw them last week, and there's no reason why any harm should come to them." He tried to sound confident, but the words came out in a croaked whisper.

WHAT NOT TO DO

- Don't use dialogue tags every time a character says something.
- Avoid dialogue tags with adverbs *(she said hoarsely, he said gratingly)*.
- Don't over-use these techniques, because they can become tedious to read. As a guideline, I suggest using no more than four tone-of-voice descriptions per scene.

PROFESSIONAL TIP

Use similes to reveal something about the characters' background or the current situation, for world-building or to foreshadow things to come. This needs creative thought but is amazingly effective in a subtle way.

Here are some examples how I used this trick in my books.

Her voice had the low hum of an arrow in flight. (Emotion: This character is tense and determined. World-building: This novel is set in a world where people use bows and arrows. Foreshadowing: There will be a battle where the characters shoot arrows.)

Kirral's voice had the soft scraping tone of a sword grinding against a whetstone. (Emotion: This character is feeling increasingly aggressive, and he's still holding back. World-building: The novel is set in historical fantasy world where people fight with swords. Foreshadowing: This harmless-seeming character is more dangerous than he appears.)

See if you can create similes which describe the tone of the character's voice, convey his emotions and hint at something you want the reader to know, in a way that suits your book, your genre and your personal author voice.

ASSIGNMENT

Take a scene you have written, perhaps one that's already well revised. Find one instance where a non-PoV character says something that you want to have more impact. What does this character feel while he's saying this? Insert a brief description of the tone of his voice, perhaps with a creative simile.

CHAPTER 5: THOUGHTS

Pouring the character's thoughts on paper is the easiest way to show what he feels.

'This is hopeless. I can't go on.'
'I hope John likes me in this dress.'
'Mary is such an irritating bore.'

The simplicity of this method is attractive to novice writers, many of whom use it clumsily or too much.

Here are some techniques to make it work:

1. Keep thoughts short - a few words rather than several sentences.

Here's a thought penned by an inexperienced writer:

I wonder what would be the best thing to do in this situation. I really don't know what, because there doesn't seem to be an obvious solution, but I have to do something, and it's up to me to decide what.

This is how a professional author writes it:

What now?

2. Thoughts don't need dialogue tags *(she thought, he wondered, she realised, he mused)* unless it's unclear who does the thinking. The thoughts will feel more immediate to the reader without tags. This may require changing the tenses.

Instead of

"This is getting dangerous," she thought.

Write

This was getting dangerous.

Instead of

"I won't go on a date with this irritating bore again," I decided.

Write

I wouldn't go on another date with this irritating bore.

Or

I decided not to go on another date with this irritating bore.

3. Use Direct Speech rather than Indirect Speech. Although Indirect Speech is correct, it can feel detached and stilted.

Instead of

She contemplated whether the rope ladder would hold.

Write

Would the rope ladder hold?

Instead of

He assumed that Cordelia would come to his rescue soon.

Write

Cordelia would come to his rescue soon.

4. Use fewer thoughts in third-person stories than in first-person narratives, and fewer in omniscient PoV than in deep PoV fiction.

The punctuation and formatting rules for thoughts vary from country to country and from publisher to publisher. Some publishers want thoughts enclosed by single quote marks, others by doubles, yet others want no quote marks at all. Some like thoughts rendered in italics, others find italics unacceptable. Don't worry about this.

WHAT NOT TO DO

Don't show the thoughts of a character who is not the PoV at that moment.

If you apply tags, avoid unnecessary words. When I was editing magazines, I often received beginner submissions with tags like this:

'All is lost,' I thought to myself in my head.

This could easily be tightened to

'All is lost,' I thought.

Actually, in most cases, it would be enough to write

All was lost.

PROFESSIONAL TIP

Thoughts have a pace-slowing effect. Use them sparingly (or not at all) in sections where you want the pace to be fast, such as in fight and chase scenes.

The reverse also works. Insert thoughts wherever you want to slow the pace, for example, during the PoV's enforced inactivity, or while he's desperately waiting for someone who doesn't arrive.

ASSIGNMENTS

1. Working with a draft manuscript, find a section where you have conveyed a character's thoughts. Pare the thoughts down to the shortest possible version.

2. Put yourself in the mind of the PoV character of the scene you plan to write next. What does she feel? What thoughts go through her mind, reflecting the main emotion? How can you condense these thoughts into a single brief sentence?

CHAPTER 6:
DESCRIPTIONS CONVEY MOOD

In this chapter, I'll show you how you can subtly convey how the PoV character feels, and at the same time manipulate the reader's emotions.

When you describe something, use words that evoke emotional connotations. Focus especially on verbs.

Here several sentences describing dusk. Each reflects a different emotion in the PoV and evokes a different mood in the reader.

Sunset gilded the horizon.
The sky bruised into night.
The sun dropped, taking the last remaining warmth with it.
The horizon throbbed crimson, then gentled to a soft pink.
Thick clouds hung on the horizon, and only a watery strip of orange peeked through.
The sun set, leaving a red-gashing wound between the earth and the sky.
The sky was sliding into dour night.
The day was already dying. Dusk hung like a purple mist.
The clouds at the horizon darkened. A sliver of the sinking sun glinted in their folds.
Sundown bloodied the horizon.
The sky flared up in hues of crimson and purple.
The last sliver of sunlight vanished from the sky.
Darkness came down like a hood.
The sun sank to rest behind the wagon track.
Within minutes, the fierce colours faded to pale.
Wind-ruffled pink clouds drifted along the horizon.
The sun slipped behind the dunes and cast a golden veil across their shifting shapes.
The sun painted a last, brilliant orange streak across the jagged mountain.
The sun died in streaks of gold and purple.

As you can see, there are many ways to describe a sunset. Obviously, not every one of these would suit every story and every writing style.

I've already used some of these in my novels, so if you want a sunset, don't copy my phrases but create your own mood-rich descriptions.

Here's another example. The PoV character sees another person who wears a gold choker around her neck.

Instead of simply stating

She wore a gold choker around her neck.

Try to convey how the PoV character feels about this woman, about the necklace, or about the situation in general. You might choose one of these:

A gold choker clawed at her neck.
A gold choker embraced her neck.
A gold choker caressed her neck.
A gold choker glinted around her neck.
A gold choker slithered around her neck.
A gold choker sparkled around her neck.
A gold choker snaked around her neck.

To convey or create positive emotions such as joy, hope and happiness, use positive verbs like *sparkle, dance, lap, skip, embrace, hug, shine, bloom, crown, caress.*

For dark moods and emotions, use verbs with negative connotations, such as *slash, rob, claw, stab, stump, steal, slither, scratch, dump, boil, scrape, squash, struggle, beg, clutch, grasp, devour, squeeze.*

WHAT NOT TO DO

Don't use in-your-face metaphors for descriptions. If the PoV character feels depressed, don't show heavy clouds in the sky. If she's desperate, don't show starving children in ragged clothes, and if she's happy, don't show a field of frolicking lambs. The effect would be melodramatic. Although melodrama has its uses in some kinds of fiction, most novels are better without it.

Beginners are prone to this mistake, especially when describing the weather. In novice-written stories it always rains when the character feels sad, and when she feels cheerful, the sun shines. In literary criticism, this is called a 'pathetic fallacy'.

For a subtler effect without melodrama, choose weather conditions, landscapes and objects which don't reflect the emotion - but evoke the mood through your word choices.

Your happy character may see ragged children on a litter-strewn pavement, and you can describe this in a positive way by using words like *play, fun, laugh, dance, skip*. An unhappy character may see a garden arch covered in roses, and through her filter of experience it's a depressing sight if you use words like *smother, cling, snake, droop*.

PROFESSIONAL TIP

Use descriptions conveying emotions to foreshadow future plot events and to hint at things you don't spell out.

Perhaps it's evening, and one of the characters says she has to go home to her husband. She says it in a subdued voice, and her eyes have lost their sparkle. The readers understand that this woman doesn't look forward to spending the evening with that man, but don't know what's wrong. If you now insert a description of the sunset - *The sky bruised into night* - the readers will grasp on a subconscious level that the husband is a brutal man whose violence she fears.

If you choose to try this professional-level technique in your fiction, apply it with a light brush, so that readers are not consciously aware of what you are doing.

ASSIGNMENTS

1. Does your work-in-progress (WiP) have a scene which takes place in the evening? Consider how the PoV character feels. Write a sentence describing the sunset (or dusk, lights-out, descending darkness or other evening feature) with words that convey his emotions. Use the list of examples in this chapter as inspiration, without copying them. If your WiP has no evening scene at all, write about sunrise or high noon instead.

2. In a scene you are planning or revising, identify the PoV character's main emotion. Now consider the time of the day and the weather, and visualise the surroundings. How do they look, viewed through the filter of how the PoV character feels?

CHAPTER 7:
SIMILES

In this chapter, I'll share a technique that's highly effective. But you need to think carefully about how, when and how much to use it.

A simile is a comparison. You describe something by comparing it with something else. In fiction, you compare something the PoV character experiences (sees, hears, smells, touches, feels, senses...) for the first time with something he has experienced previously.

Let's say the PoV is John, an elderly man with a chequered past. He visits Mrs Brown who shows him into her drawing room. You might use a simile like these:

The drawing room looked and smelled like a brothel, overloaded with burgundy velvet and musky perfumes.

The drawing room was as stark and sterile as a prison's reception room.

The mantel displayed more kitschy knick-knacks than a church bazaar.

The chair was as hard and rigid as the lady herself.

The air was heavy with the smell of mould and mothballs, as if Mrs Brown had not bothered to open a window since Princess Diana's death.

Each of these paints a different picture, but they all imply that he dislikes both Mrs Brown and her drawing room.

The two parts are often linked with 'like', 'as if', 'than', 'as...as', 'reminiscent of' or other constructions. (Depending on which dictionary you consult, you may broader or narrower definitions of the word 'simile'. Don't let the differences confuse you, because for the purpose of this writing technique they don't matter.)

Well-chosen similes can provide many things at once:

1. An impression of the current object or experience
2. A clue about the PoV's attitude
3. World-building information
4. Information about the PoV's background (job, skills, childhood, interests etc.)
5. Humour (optional)
6. A clue about the PoV's emotions
7. Planting an emotion in the reader's subconscious

We've already looked at how to use similes to describe a character's voice. You can also use them to create places, smells, objects, movements, facial features and more.

Decide what emotion you wish to convey: sad, frightened, disgusted, happy or pleased? Then choose something the PoV experiences in that moment, and compare it with something sad, frightening, disgusting, happy or pleasant from the PoV's memory. (Instead of a real memory, you can also draw on the PoV's imagination, although this disables some of the simile's benefits.)

WHAT NOT TO DO

Don't use similes drawing on something outside the PoV's experience and imagination. For example, don't say that the breeze stinging the PoV's cheeks is as freezing as the wind in the Antarctic if the PoV has never been to the Antarctic, or that a girl's figure is as slender as Audrey Hepburn's if your historical story takes place before Audrey Hepburn was born.

PROFESSIONAL TIP

The way you use similes is part of your unique author voice. Here you need to make an artistic decision about how many to use, and in what style. Some authors create many similes to enrich their writing, others use almost none. Some apply similes so deftly that the reader chuckles at the funny quips, others so subtly that the reader isn't even aware of them.

The choice depends on the genre as well as on your personal taste. Thrillers, for example, are traditionally rich in vivid similes. Many thriller writers past and present display a brilliant mastery of startling and witty similes, but this doesn't mean you have to imitate them. The choice is yours.

ASSIGNMENT

Take a scene you're currently working on, perhaps one for which you have a rough draft already. Select something or someone the PoV character experiences for the first time - maybe a new colleague, his wife's latest dress, his enemy's swagger, the hotel's ballroom, the live band in the club, the Chinese meal his mate has cooked.

Now put yourself deep into the PoV character's mind. How does he feel about this person or object? How does he generally feel at this moment?

Compare the new thing to something the PoV has experienced before. Choose a simile that conveys the PoV's emotion.

You may want to write down several ideas, and wait a couple of days before choosing the one you like best.

CHAPTER 8:
SECRET, SUPPRESSED AND FAKED FEELINGS

In this chapter, I'll discuss the trickiest kind of emotions to write - those that the character doesn't admit to. The techniques are for advanced-level writers, so if you find them too difficult, feel free to skip this chapter and return to it later when you have more experience.

SUPPRESSED EMOTIONS

When a character doesn't like what she feels, she may deny those feelings to herself, or she may consciously fight them.

1. Consciously suppressed emotions

If she's conscious of the feelings she wants to suppress, she'll seek to put a different, acceptable emotion on top.

She may do this with self talk, for example: *"I can do this." "Ghosts don't exist." "I know that my husband is faithful."*

She may also deliberately change her posture, tone of voice or facial expression, mimicking the body language of the emotion she wants to feel.

If Mary feels discouraged, but doesn't allow herself this emotion, she mimics the body language of resolution: *Mary straightened her spine. Mary raised her chin. She squared her shoulders.*

If she wants to suppress sadness, she may imitate a cheerful mood: *Mary forced a smile. Mary injected her voice with a note of cheer.*

If she's angry and wants to feel serene, you could write: *Mary willed her jaw to unclench. She counted ten breaths.*

The self-talk works only for the PoV character, while the body language works for PoV and non-PoV characters alike.

2. Denial

When a character denies what he feels, he is not even consciously aware of this emotion. This poses a challenge for the writer. I recommend treating this with a delicate touch. The clues you give the reader have to be so subtle that they're barely there.

For the PoV character, give the barest hint of a physical sensation - a body part itching, a stiffening of the neck, a faint headache. a slight discomfort in the seating position.

You can also show a stronger physical sensation, and have the PoV character attribute it to a different cause.

Suppose Mary hears news that's seriously scary, but she doesn't want to acknowledge the danger, let alone feel afraid. Her subconscious mind understands the danger signals, and sends goose-pimples across Mary's arms. Her conscious mind, however, doesn't want to admit this and seeks another explanation. *The evening sun was sinking fast, and the air chilled. Mary wrapped herself in her cardigan.*

If the non-PoV character is in denial, use involuntary body language, the kind over which people have no control. Changes in facial skin colour work well for this: *Her face paled. Her cheeks flushed.*

This is the immediate reaction. The character may follow them almost at once with different, conscious body language cue in order to demonstrate to herself and others that she feels the opposite.

Such hints are extremely subtle, and most readers won't consciously perceive them... but their subconscious minds will.

SECRET EMOTIONS

A character may be comfortable with his own feelings, but not want others guess them. Perhaps the display of emotion would not be appropriate, or it would offend the other person.

The best way to show this is with 'corrected' body language. The character reacts with facial expression or gesture that comes natural in the situation, then catches what he's doing and stops it at once.

Here are three examples for this technique:

John learns that his boss's child is terminally ill and slowly dying. Feeling deep compassion, John's immediate reaction is to reach out and give the man a hug. But he immediately checks himself. Hugging another man, especially the boss, is not appropriate, so he stops the movement and takes a step back.

Or maybe John is a grunt soldier in the army. His sergeant, a nasty bully, steps close to John and yells an insult into his face. John is furious, and his natural instinct is to punch the man in the face. His right hand balls into a fist. But his discipline wins over his emotion. He controls himself, unclenches his fist, and says 'Yes, sir.'

If Mary learns that she has won the coveted job promotion, she feels triumphant, and this shows in her tall posture, proudly lifted head and big beaming smile. Then she remembers that both the managing director and the two failed candidates are present, and that a display of triumph would be inappropriate, so she quickly lowers her eyes and curbs her smile to one of modest pleasure.

Another way to show secret emotions is with the character's voice. The voice may rise or drop in pitch or volume. Since people try not to give away their feelings with their voices, they may clear their throats or cough a little before they speak.

Readers will understand these cues, and wait for the time when the character does act on his emotions, for example, when John, unrestrained by army discipline, punches the bullying sergeant in the face, or when he hugs another man regardless of convention.

FAKED FEELINGS

A character may need to fake an emotion he doesn't really feel. The reasons for this can be noble or despicable. Perhaps he must pretend to admire the cruel dictator, to save himself and his family from execution. Maybe he pretends to love his aunt, so she'll name him heir to her fortune.

When my characters pretend emotions they don't truly feel, I have fun writing this.

My favourite technique is to create contradictions. The character's words claim a feeling, but his body language gives him away.

Perhaps Mary tells John that she loves him, but she doesn't meet his eyes and leans slightly away from him.

Or John claims that he doesn't fear vampires, but he glances at the rapidly sinking sun and walks faster.

A more subtle variant is to have two body language cues contradict each other. The character deliberately uses postures and movements that convey his faked emotions, but his body produces symptoms that are outside his control.

Let's say Mary waits in the reception area to be called in for a job interview. Knowing that she will be watched, she pretends serene confidence. She manages to keep her shoulders relaxed and to hold her hands still on her lap... but sweat trickles down her temples, and her legs constantly cross and uncross.

Fake smiles can be easy to spot. If a character pretends pleasure, the mouth curves higher up on one side of the face than on the other, the eyes don't shine and the corners of the eyes don't crinkle.

For a non-PoV character, you can write:

John's lips curved, but the smile did not reach his eyes.

Or, less obvious:

John's lips curved.

Since there relatively few body language cues to reveal faked emotions, it can be difficult to find fresh ones. Take care not to use the same cues repeatedly in your novel.

For the PoV character, you need to use a different approach, because she obviously won't be aware of the body language signals she's inadvertently sending. I recommend focusing on the PoV character's effort instead:

John forced a smile.

John composed his features, aiming for the noble sacrifice expression of Humphrey Bogart in Casablanca. "I will always love you, but we must part."

WHAT NOT TO DO

When a character suppresses anxiety or nervousness, novices tend to write *'She took a deep breath to steady herself'* or *'He exhaled slowly.'* That's fine once or twice in the book, but in many novice-penned manuscripts the characters take deep breaths and exhale slowly in every chapter, and that gets tedious fast.

PROFESSIONAL TIP

For consciously suppressed emotions, combine the body language cue with self-talk. The self-talk can be in direct or indirect speech, but keep it short.

Mary squared her shoulders. "Someone is bound to give me a job."

Mary raised her chin. She would try again tomorrow.

ASSIGNMENTS

Try the following exercises to test how well you've grasped this challenging lesson. If you find them too difficult, skip them for now and return to them later when you feel ready.

1. Find a situation in your WiP where the PoV character hides, pretends or suppresses an emotion. Convey this in one or two

sentences. Use whichever of the suggested methods suits your story best.

2. Now do the same with a non-PoV character.

CHAPTER 9:
VARYING THE EMOTIONAL INTENSITY

Feelings aren't static. They rise and subside, flare up and simmer. Make your scene more interesting and realistic by varying the intensity of the emotions.

Here are two methods.

1. Use different shades of the same emotion.

Here are two examples.

At the beginning of the scene, the PoV character feels annoyance. This builds to anger and finally escalates to fury.

In a scary scene, the PoV character feels apprehension at first, then fear. For a while, she experiences sheer terror. Then the danger passes, and the terror gives way to dread because she knows the monster will be back.

2. Cluster cues.

A single visceral response or body language cue indicates a mild feeling. When the emotion gets intense, insert several visceral responses or body language cues close together.

Here are three variations of the same sentence showing Mary's fear, with one, two and three visceral responses. As you can see, the one with three is the most intense.

Mary's mouth went dry.
Mary's mouth went dry and her heart thumped.
Mary's mouth went dry, her heart thumped, and the hair lifted on the nape of her neck.

For intense emotions, you can combine the visceral reactions and body language cues in a single sentence, like in the above example, or insert them separately, as long as they are close together. Here's an example:

Mary's mouth went dry and her heart thumped. On the other side of the room, an invisible hand turned the key in its lock. Metal scraped softly. The hair lifted on the nape of her neck.

WHAT NOT TO DO

Don't keep the PoV character's emotion at the same level. The result would be unrealistic and boring.

PROFESSIONAL TIP

The human mind can't sustain intense emotions (such as terror and elation) for a long time. This applies to the reader's feelings as well as the character's.

Instead of trying to prolong the emotional intensity, let it relax for a bit. The terror may subside to dread, and the elation to satisfaction. After a few paragraphs, you can turn the intensity to full volume again.

ASSIGNMENT

1. In the scene you're currently writing, what is the PoV character's main emotion? Identify where the feeling begins, where it grows significantly, and where it reaches its full height. Convey the feeling and its intensity by using visceral responses.

2. Either in the same scene or in one for which you've recently written a draft, look at the most important character after the PoV. What does this person feel? Identify one section where his emotion is mild, and another where this emotion is strong. Write a sentence for each, using body language cues.

CHAPTER 10:
LAYERING EMOTIONS

Humans are complex creatures, and we have several emotions in a short time, often at once. Even when one emotion dominates our thoughts, others are coursing beneath the surface. Give your characters - especially the main characters - several emotions in each scene.

The emotions can follow one after another, and they can also overlap.

Let's say Mary visits a classmate from school she hasn't met for twenty years. While Mary struggles to earn a living flipping burgers in a fast food joint, Sue has built a successful career and lives in a luxurious mansion. You write the scene of this visit.

What does Mary feel? Perhaps initially there is curiosity about how Sue is doing these days, followed by surprise when she realises that her old classmate lives in such wealthy surroundings. Maybe there's awe at the magnificence of the house, and trepidation as Mary wonders if she has dressed too casually. Later, Mary may feel envy, because Sue has the lifestyle she craves, and resentment, because Mary has to do a drudge job while fortune has fallen into Sue's lap. When the butler serves lunch, Mary feels worry about etiquette because she doesn't know how to eat oysters properly, and embarrassment when she spills the sauce on the tablecloth. Her resentment intensifies when she thinks of how much the oysters cost - she could feed her children for a week on that money.

Then they talk about life. Mary feels embarrassment to admit what she does for a living, and surprise when she learns that Sue had also worked in a fast food joint for five years. Her surprise intensifies when she finds out that life was far from pleasant for Sue - ditched by her boyfriend when she was pregnant, single motherhood, fired from her job because of her allegedly immoral lifestyle, then marriage to an addict who stole the housekeeping money to spend on drugs, a second child born brain-damaged, her first child permanently crippled after a car accident...

Now Mary feels compassion. She also feels ashamed for her earlier resentment, and gratitude that her own children are able-bodied and healthy.

A little later she finds out how Sue worked herself out of this morass, got a grip on her alcoholism, supported her children working ten hours a day, took evening classes to educate herself, got a job, worked hard, gained promotion, worked her way into management... Disbelief flares up, then gives way to admiration. The envy and resentment have vanished.

By the time the butler clears the table, Mary feels intense admiration. She also feels hope that she too may be able to rise from her dead-end poverty. When she leaves, a new emotion grows in her: determination. She is determined to work her way to success.

That's a great number of emotions, isn't it?

You don't need to use quite as many in your scene, but you may.

How many emotions should you include in a scene? While I don't want to make rules, here is a guideline you may wish to follow.

Point-of-view character: at least four emotions.
Second-most important character: three or more emotions.
Minor characters: two emotions each.
Walk-on characters: one emotion each.

WHAT NOT TO DO

Don't write a scene in which the PoV character (or another major character) has only one single emotion. That would feel flat.

PROFESSIONAL TIP

When planning the scene, write down the emotions the major characters feel. This will make the writing much easier.

To keep track of the emotional choreography, find a way to represent the emotions visually. Perhaps you want to use comment boxes in the margin of the draft manuscript, or create a spreadsheet where every plot event has a line and every emotion a differently-coloured column.

ASSIGNMENT

Think of the scene you're planning to write. Identify at least four emotions the PoV character will feel, and at least three emotions for the next most important character.

CHAPTER 11:
STIRRING READER EMOTIONS

A reader who feels moved by a book will read it again, tell others about it, recommend it to her reading circle and remember it for the rest of her life. If you can arouse strong emotions in the readers, your book will be success.

Here are five methods to achieve this.

1. Get deep into the PoV's experience.

This is the most important method. The reader experiences events through the filter of the PoV character. If you handle this skilfully, what the PoV feels is what the reader feels.

Pay special attention to visceral responses (see Chapter 2), thoughts (Chapter 5) and descriptions (Chapter 6).

Showing the scene through one character's PoV has more emotional impact than omniscient PoV.

2. Trigger the reader's own memories.

Readers respond most strongly when what happens in the book evokes an emotional situation from their own life.

A reader who has had to live in a flat where the heating has broken down leading to weeks of ice cold rooms, damp seeped through the walls and mould crept across the wallpaper because the landlord ignored complaints, will immediately feel the exasperation, anger and despair of a PoV who has a neglectful landlord.

Readers remember the mix of insecurity and heady excitement of going on their first date, the nervous yet hopeful thrill when opening the letter that may contain the job offer, the painfully mounting suspicion that their partner is cheating on them.

Writing Vivid Emotions

The situations in the novel don't need to be exactly the same, as long as they are related and evoke intense emotions.

Consider this when developing your novel plot or planning a scene: what similar dilemmas and emotional upheavals has the typical reader experienced?

This depends of course on your target audience. If you write YA (young adult = fiction for teenagers), most readers will know what it's like to have a crush on boy who doesn't requite their interest, how it feels to be excluded from the group they desperately want to belong to, and how much it hurts when the girl they thought was their best friend betrays them. However, they won't have experienced the joys and pains of parenthood and grief at the death of a spouse.

3. Use smells.

This is a micro method to trigger emotions instantly. No other sense evokes emotions as strongly as the sense of smell. Mention what a person smells like, and the reader will immediately like or dislike her. Describe the odours of a place, and the reader will feel relaxed or disgusted.

A single sentence is all that's needed. Here are some examples:

The room smelled of jasmine tea and freshly baked bread.
The room smelled sharply of disinfectant, carbolic soap and bleach.
The room smelled of stale cigarette smoke, rotting fruit and piss.

4. Use description to send subconscious signals.

This technique overlaps with what I suggested in Chapter 6, but is subtler and needs to be applied with greater skill.

In Chapter 6, we looked at filtering the descriptions through the PoV character's perceptions, revealing how she feels about places, objects and people. You can also use phrases that trigger emotions in the reader only - emotions the PoV doesn't share.

To do this, compose the description so it largely matches the PoV's feelings - but make a few subtle word-choices that evoke what you want the reader to feel.

Here's an example. Let's say PoV character Mary has a date with John, whom she doesn't know well but who she hopes is Mr Right. As they walk along the beach, she's in love, feeling tenderness, hope, and a whole host of romantic emotions.

Here is a description of the sunset beach in romantic terms to convey Mary's love-hazed perspective:

Waves lapped at the beach, caressing the pebbles. The leaves of the palm trees whispered as they brushed against one another. The sun touched the horizon, warming the clouds with a golden-pink glow.

Here is a different version. It still shows Mary's romantic perception, but it also sends a danger signal. The hint is so subtle that Mary won't perceive it, but the reader will, at least on a subconscious level:

Waves lapped at the beach, caressing the pebbles. The leaves of the palm trees whispered as they brushed against one another. The sun touched the horizon, and golden-pink clouds covered the bruise-purple sky.

Now the reader feels something the PoV does not: apprehension.

5. Tell the reader more than the PoV knows.

If you're writing in deep PoV, this is difficult to achieve. The solution is to plant several hints in a way that allows the PoV character to ignore them, while the reader picks them up.

Suppose Mary believes that her new lover John is single and has never been married. When they drink champagne on his lawn, describe what the surrounding garden looks like: large-flowered pink clematis winding through camellia bushes, young apples forming on fruit trees, a child's skipping rope curled like a snake under the hedge, a spade and fork leaning against the shed, and climbing roses spreading a sweet heady scent. Mary sees the child's skipping rope, but doesn't consciously register it among the other items.

If you plant a few more hints - say, Johns familiarity with marital and parenting matters, and the flagon of Chanel No 5 in his bathroom cabinet - the reader's subconscious will add up these discrepancies and create an emotion Mary herself doesn't yet feel: doubt.

Dialogue is another great tool for this. Suppose you want Mary to trust her fiancé John and to discover only several chapters later, when they're on their honeymoon, that he is a violent man.

To do this, weave phrases and metaphors of violence into John's dialogue. As a businessman, he talks about crushing his competitors, stamping out rumours, slashing prices.

You can also have him talk about how he punched the guy who insulted is mother with lewd remarks, how as a fourteen-year-old he beat up the boy who tried to rape his sister, how he caught and beat up a burglar. He reckons his violence in these situations was justified, and Mary thinks so too. She even admires his courage and assertiveness. But the reader will notice that there were quite a few incidents of violence, and feels apprehension.

WHAT NOT TO DO

Don't leave the PoV to tell the reader the truth outright. Avoid sentences like these:

Mary was too in love to suspect that John had a wife already.
Mary failed to realise until much later that John enjoyed violence.

One emotion you should never evoke in the reader is boredom, even if the PoV feels bored. You don't want your reader to feel bored while reading your book.

PROFESSIONAL TIP

For the most intense emotional experience, tell the whole story from the same PoV. This allows the reader to identify so fully with the PoV character that she becomes that person. Changing the PoV from scene to scene or from chapter to chapter doesn't create the same level of identification, and the reader's emotions won't be as strong.

ASSIGNMENT

In your manuscript draft, find a section where you want the reader to like or dislike someone or something. Insert a mention of a smell to create that feeling.

CHAPTER 12:
THESAURUS OF BODY LANGUAGE CUES

I've compiled some of the most common emotions characters feel in fiction, with typical cues conveying those feelings. These will help you go beyond the novice limits of 'she smiled' and 'he frowned'.

Of course you won't find every emotion on the human spectrum here, but in many cases you'll see something you can use to reveal a non-PoV character's feelings. Some of them are conscious tells and suitable for the PoV as well.

Use this thesaurus when you want a quick cue to get a point across, or as a starting point for more thorough research.

Write the body language cues creatively, clothing them in words which suit your author voice.

Anger, Fury, Rage

Flaring nostrils, glaring eyes, staring, noisy breathing, pounding palm or fist on the table, balling hands into fists, slamming a door or drawer, throwing/slamming/pushing things down instead of placing them gently, face goes red, mottled skin, standing with legs apart and hands balled into fists on either side of the waist, stomping a foot down, crossed arms, large gestures with the arms, voice getting louder, yelling, harsh laugh, lips pulled back showing teeth, nostrils flare, jabbing a finger at the other person's face.

Anxiety, Nervousness

Adjusting or pulling at shirt/jacket cuffs, repeatedly glancing at wristwatch, winding up watch unnecessarily, straightening neck-tie, twiddling with necklace, pulling at/loosening collar, gnawing lips, biting finger nails, rolling one's shoulders, rubbing the back of one's neck, scratching, repeatedly checking the phone, repeatedly glancing at the door, rubbing palms together, lips so tightly pressed together they almost disappear, interlaced fingers rubbing up and down, stroking a palm with a finger of the other hand, jerky movements, checking one's wallet, voice higher than normal, small gestures

Apprehension, Dread

Arms clutched to the chest, rubbing palms along thighs, holding hands on abdomen, trembling hands, nail-biting, biting the inside of the cheek, gnawing at lips, sweating, voice higher than normal, small gestures, walking with dragging footsteps, both shoulders lean forward so the chest forms a hollow.

Boredom

Yawning, looking at one's watch, watching a clock, sitting with the face resting in one's hand, wandering gaze, doodling on paper, eyes downcast, starts doing something else

Confusion

Rubbing a hand across the forehead, frowning, fumbling, grimacing, a slight head-shake with an open mouth, blank looks, running hands through the hair, narrowing eyes, tilted head.

Contempt

Corners of the mouth turned down, the lower lip juts forward, stiff posture, nose turning up, rolling the eyes, slight quivering of the nostrils as if smelling something bad, nostrils contracting, leaning back with arms crossed, looking down one's nose, picking fluff of one's clothes.

Curiosity

Tilting head sidewards, blinking, body posture perking up, lifting eyebrows, watching intently, pushing glasses up on the nose, bending or leaning to get closer, nodding slowly, lips parting slightly.

Desire

Wide eyes, large pupils, parting lips, voice lowers, increase swallowing, stroking one's own throat, soft gaze, shining eyes, touching one's own lips

Determination

Raised chin, straight posture, fast steps, chest thrust out, firm handshake, leaning forward, pushing up one's sleeves.

Disappointment

Slumping shoulders, hunched posture, lowering the head, lips pressing together, a bitter smile, heavy sighs, mouth falling open, shuffling feet, eyes closing, fluttering hands, voice going lower and quieter, pressing hand to abdomen, pressing hands to temples.

Disbelief

Widening eyes, frowning and raising brows at the same time, mouth opening and closing, hands dropping to one's side, rapid blinking, raising one eyebrow, brief head shake, tugging at the earlobe, scratching the jaw, rubbing the forehead.

Disgust

Taking a step away, leaning away, head pulls back, nostrils twitch, rubbing the hands as if washing them, small cough, choking noise in the throat, covering the mouth, eyebrows lower and pull together.

Doubt, Suspicion

Pressing lips together, shuffling feet, pacing, eyes narrow, frowning, avoiding eye-contact, darting quick glances at the object or person, raised eyebrows, pursed lips, lips pressed flat together, head-shake, crossing the arms, swaying from side to side, fake smile, biting inside of the lip, rubbing earlobes.

Eagerness

Eyes shine, leaning forward, moving (walking, running) fast towards the point, pulling chair closer to the table, head lifted, animated gestures.

Embarrassment, Shame

Chest caves in, head droops, rubbing the back of one's neck, pulling at one's collar, weak voice, looking down, avoiding eye contact, red face, ears turn red, head-shakes, lips pressed together, feet shuffling, the spine curls, hiding one's face behind a book or magazine, stuttering, trembling chin, blank look, 'crumpling' onto a chair, slouching posture while sitting or walking.

Envy

Staring, mouth thins, lips part slightly, swallowing frequently, hands clench into fists, touching (perhaps pinching) one's throat, hands twitch.

Excitement

Hands clasped between breasts, fast strides, eye contact with others, ruddy cheeks, bouncing from foot to foot, throaty laughter, giggling, trembling, large waving gestures.

Fear, Terror

Shrill voice, whispering, looking all around including behind, jerky movements, flinching at noises, lips and chin trembling, small gestures, face pale or ashen, goose-pimples, shaking hands, shaking all over, pressing palms or fists to the side of one's head, sweating heavily, clasping someone or something, hugging oneself, rapid blinking.

Frustration

Stiff posture, rushed speech, pinched lips, squinting, hands clasped behind one's back, arms crossed in front of the chest, pinched expression, rubbing the back of one's neck, tapping fingers on the table.

Gratitude

Soft-glowing eyes, a smile that starts small and spreads across the whole face, holding a handshake for longer than normal, holding palms in open position, placing hand on one's chest.

Guilt

Averted or lowered gaze, blushing, rubbing one's ear or nose, pulling at one's collar, voice cracks, stuttering, shoulders drawn up, elbows tucked close to body, becoming unnaturally still with almost no movement.

Happiness, Elation

Babbling, rapid talking, a beaming smile that doesn't stop, a big grin, flushed face, shining eyes, chest thrust forward, throwing something in the air and catching it, running, skipping, dancing, tilting head back and looking skywards, spontaneous hugs and kisses, enthusiastic waving,

Hatred

Shaking fists, holding fingers tense and curled like claws, bared teeth, nostrils flare, shaking voice, veins throb visibly on the face or neck, squared shoulders.

Hope

Shining face, wiggling, squirming, strong eye contact, leaning forward, shifting back and forth, lips slightly parted, raking teeth across the lips without biting hard.

Hurt

Eyes widen, forehead furrows, mouth opens, colour drains from face, tears form in the eyes but don't run down the cheek, slow headshake, clutching one's stomach, hanging one's head.

Impatience

Feet jiggling or bouncing, one foot tapping, one or both knees bumping up and down, glancing repeatedly at one's watch or at a clock, popping one's knuckles, chewing the bottom lip, rocking back and forth, fingers drumming on the desk, interlacing fingers and rolling wrists back and forth, massaging one's temples, changing position from standing to sitting and back, pacing.

Irritation, Annoyance

Sharp tone, clipped replies, voice getting louder, slapping and pushing things down instead of placing them gently, crossing and uncrossing the legs, grimacing, frowning, lips pressed into a thin line, arms folded across the chest, looking upwards, rolling eyes, hard smile.

Jealousy

Stares, whiny voice, flushed cheeks, small quick movements, lips pressed flat or pursed, sullen facial expression, pinched face, spitting (in direction of the rival), kicking at objects on the ground.

Love

Beaming face, glowing cheeks, moving close to the person, staying close, gazing at the person, long intense eye contact, licking one's lips, bouncing steps when walking, smiling a lot.

Pride

Chin raised, shoulders back, chest pushed forward, gleaming eyes, satisfied smile, straight posture, booming laugh, knowing grin, using hand to comb or flick hair back.

Relief

Shoulders drop, posture slumps, palm pressed to one's heart, eyes shine, slow smile, shaking laughter, lips part, mouth gapes, rocking back and forth, making the sign of the cross (if Christian), uttering a thanks to God (if religious), stumbling.

Remorse, Regret

Downturned mouth, eyes squeezed shut, eyebrows pulled together, rubbing a hand across one's face, holding a hand on one's breastbone, head-shaking, weak voice, cracking voice, breaking into sobs, grimacing, lifting hands and letting them fall, holding head in one's hands, tears run down the cheek, chin quivers.

Resentment

Staring, lips pressed together, clenched fists, narrow eyes, mouth pinched or pouting, arms crossed over the chest, sharp tone, snapping at others, hard smile, looking past the person instead of at them.

Resignation, Hopelessness

Head-shake, slumped shoulders, sagging facial features, dull eyes, shuffling walk, low monotone voice, holding one's head in both hands while sitting.

Sadness, Grief

Sniffing (especially when the lost person/object is mentioned), wiping at nose, crying, red eyes, streaks of running make-up under the eyes, sitting with the face in one's hands, sitting with the body leaning forward and the head on an arm, monotone voice, staring at one's hands, bowed posture, trembling chin, trembling lips, clutching a memento of that person, pressing a fist against the chest.

Satisfaction

Head held high, chin lifted, chest puffed out, upright posture, crisp nodding, arms stretched out wide for gestures as well as for static postures, smiling.

Shock

Rigid posture, movements stop suddenly, stiff movements, paling, staring, open mouth, hand clasped to mouth

Surprise

Eyebrows shoot up, mouth drops open, gasping or squealing, stopping in mid-movement, eyes widen, dazed look, incredulous stare, hand flies to chest, shaking the head, stuttering, barking laugh, voice rises higher.

Triumph

Throwing one or both arms up and holding them up in a muscle-emphasising pose, one or both lower arms pointing up, one or both thumbs pointing up, upright posture, hands clasped between breasts, rubbing hands, head tilted back, open-mouthed smile showing teeth, chin raised, loud cheery voice, big gestures, slapping the other person on the back.

Unhappiness, Dejection, Depression

Vacant stare, slow lethargic movements, sitting with the head resting in one hand, sobbing, crying.

Worry

Shoulders drawn up to ears, stooped posture, rubbing one's eyebrows, jerky movements, fists clenching, rubbing wrists down the side of one's abdomen or along the thighs, head held low, pacing, wrinkled forehead.

CHAPTER 13:
THESAURUS OF VISCERAL RESPONSES

Here's a list of emotions and the physical sensations which go with them, useful for showing what the PoV character feels. (See Chapter 2 for techniques.)

You'll find fewer suggestions here than in the Thesaurus of Body Language Tells, because the range of common visceral responses is smaller. Be careful not to repeat the same sensation over and over in your book.

I recommend treating this list as a base, and expanding it by drawing on your personal experience, research and imagination. You may want to collect many visceral responses of the type your genre needs most. For example, if you're a horror writer, it's worth compiling every possibly symptom of fear, anxiety, horror, terror, apprehension, dread, shock and panic, while romance author will focus the sensations of love, tenderness, jealousy and passion in many variations, and an erotica writer needs a wide range of expressions of sexual desire.

To find more body language cues and visceral responses, you can search the internet and consult books on how to read body language, although those are typically structured to show the 'tell' and then explain what it means. You may have to compile cues and translate them backwards to build your own collection.

A more practical resource for writers is *The Emotion Thesaurus* by Angela Ackerman and Becca Puglisi. Each section covers one feeling with physical and mental responses, internal sensations and cues of suppressed emotions. I have used this reference book for years and recommend it.

Anger, Fury, Rage

Churning stomach, acid feeling in the stomach, quivering muscles in the upper arms, flushes of heat through the body, stiff neck, sweating, fast pulse, pounding heartbeat, clouded vision or flashes in one's vision, dry throat, feeling stronger than normal, feeling energetic, pounding in the ears, twitching limbs.

Anxiety, Nervousness

Thirst, tingling in the limbs, slight dizziness, churning in the stomach, contracting stomach, tightening chest, faster breathing, one's insides are 'quivering'.

Apprehension, Dread

The chest tingles, chills even when it's warm, cold fingers, goose-pimples on the skin, small hairs on the arms or at the nape of the neck rising, itching scalp, the heartbeat is heavy or sluggish, the stomach 'rolls', dizziness, shaking limbs, the bladder feels full (need to use the toilet), the throat feels tight and swallowing is difficult, the back of the throat hurts, sour taste in the mouth, a weight seems to press on the chest, wobbly knees, unpleasant cold tingle along the spine, a crawling sensation on the skin.

Boredom

Yawning, tuning out the subject matter, doodling, gazing out of the window, thinking of something else, daydreaming.

Confusion

The body grows hot, sweating, the stomach 'flutters', the chest tightens.

Contempt

Tightening chest, stiff neck, stiff jaw, heat in the abdomen.

Curiosity

Faster or stronger pulse, breath hitches.

Desire

Breathing faster, awareness of one's own heartbeat, warmth flooding the body, increased saliva, tingling all over the body or just in the hands, fingers or palms aching with the need to touch the person or object, a pang in the heart area, a pleasant shiver either just in the upper body or all over.

Determination

Stronger and slightly faster heartbeat, a 'fluttering' sensation in the chest, muscles tightening.

Disappointment

Stomach clenches, heart seems to 'shrink', heaviness in the whole body or in specific parts, the chest tightens, the breath hitches.

Disbelief

Gasping, a tingling in the chest, the stomach clenching, lightheadedness, breathing feels difficult, a momentary loss of orientation or balance.

Disgust

Choking, mouth fills with saliva combined with the urge to spit, a sour taste in the mouth, a burning in the throat, swallowing feels uncomfortable, nausea, heaving stomach, the skin 'crawls'.

Writing Vivid Emotions

Doubt, Suspicion

Heaviness in the abdomen, knotted stomach, quivering stomach, fast breath, thumping heartbeat, adrenaline rush.

Eagerness

The stomach 'flutters', a 'butterflies in the stomach' sensation, heartbeat stronger and faster, the chest expands, slight breathlessness, adrenaline rush.

Embarrassment, Shame

Need to swallow a lot, hot tingling neck and face, tight chest, stomach 'drops', lightheadedness, fast heartbeat, rushed breathing, weak knees, nausea, trembling.

Envy

Dry throat, sucking in breath through the mouth, heart beats fast, getting warm, something 'pulls' inside the stomach.

Excitement

Fast pulse, breathlessness, heightened senses, adrenaline rush, lightness in the chest, dry mouth.

Fear, Terror

Chest so tight that it hurts, stomach feels hard like a lump of rock, shaky limbs, weak legs, trying to speak but no sound comes, racing heartbeat, heart thudding so violently it threatens to burst the chest, inability to move from the spot, hypersensitivity to sounds, dizziness, clenched jaw, not feeling pain from injuries, painful chest or throat, hyperventilating, bladder feels very full, urgent need to use the toilet, bladder opens.

Frustration

Throat 'closes', stomach hardens, chest tightens, blood pressure rises, feeling warm, headache, aching shoulders and neck, painfully tense jaw.

Gratitude

Warmth all over the face and body, tingling limbs, relaxation, wide expanding chest.

Guilt

Tight chest, loss of appetite, stomach upset, thickness or pain in the throat.

Happiness, Elation

Warmth spreading throughout the body, the heart beats fast and loudly like a drum in the chest, a feeling of sunshine in one's head or chest, tingling hands, feeling alive, feeling rejuvenated, lightness in the limbs, urge to dance or skip, slight breathlessness.

Hatred

Pounding heartbeat, rising temperature, headache, muscles sore with tension, roaring in the ears, heavy loud breath, jaw aches from clenching.

Hope

A jolt through the body, tingling limbs, a 'fluttering' in the abdomen, lightheadedness, breath hitches, a sense of 'floating' above ground.

Hurt

Lungs so tight that breathing hurts, spotted vision, limbs wobbly or trembling, slow heartbeat, heart seems to stop, dizziness, hardening stomach, nausea, tight throat.

Impatience

Heavy loud breath, headache, getting warm, exhaustion.

Irritation, Annoyance

Fast pulse, tight chest, tense muscles, tight muscles in the face, twitching limbs, body temperature rises.

Jealousy

Burning sensation in the chest or the stomach, fast breath, painfully tense jaw (from clenching), hard stomach, flashes and spots in one's vision.

Love

Pulse races, the heart bangs strongly and loudly, weak knees or thighs, the tongue seems tangled in knots when one tries to speak, electrical tingling across the skin when accidentally touching the person, stomach feels hollow, fluttering in the abdomen, warmth spreads through the body when thinking of the person.

Pride

Feeling taller and stronger than before, filling the chest with deep satisfied breaths.

Relief

Sudden relaxation as pent-up tension releases, weak muscles, dry mouth, welling tears, sudden giddiness.

Remorse, Regret

Lump in the throat, runny nose, dull heavy feeling in the chest or all over the body, abdomen feels filled with knots, stomach feels weak or hard, nausea, loss of appetite, inability to sleep.

Resentment

Tightness around the chest, tight throat making it difficult to swallow, stomach pain, tense painful neck and shoulders, headache, jaw hurts from clenching.

Resignation, Hopelessness

A sensation of 'dropping' either of the hole body or the inner organs, weak muscles, numbed emotions, a sense of emptiness, lack of motivation to do anything.

Sadness, Grief

Tears welling up especially when the person or topic is mentioned, blurred vision, crying, sobbing, hot eyelids, sore or scratchy throat, the chest aches, the heart hurts like it's breaking apart, the whole body feels cold, fatigue, heavy limbs, tight chest, the world seems to move much faster or much slower than usual.

Satisfaction

Warmth spreading throughout the body, heightened awareness of other people, lightness in the chest, pleasant tiredness.

Shock

Sudden coldness starting in the body's core and spreading, heaviness in the stomach, disorientation, dizziness, weak knees, nausea, cold sweats, racing heartbeat, seeing some things with utter clarity and others blurred.

Surprise

Tingling skin, fast heartbeat, breathlessness, fluttering in the abdomen, adrenaline rush, dizziness.

Triumph

Feeling taller than usual, chest expands, warmth spreads through the body, energy surges.

Unhappiness, Dejection, Depression

Slow pulse, hollowness in the chest, aching muscles, shallow breathing, fatigue, mental and physical tiredness,

Worry

Dry mouth, tight throat, loss of appetite, sensitive stomach with digestive problems, a weight pressing down on one's chest and shoulders, headaches.

CHAPTER 14:
TWO SAMPLE STORIES

To show you how the techniques from this book work in practice, I've included two short stories. They are my own stories, so I'm free to share them with you without copyright complications. Like most of my fiction, these tales have a dark and creepy slant, so be prepared.

As you read them, watch out for emotions - the PoV character's, other characters', and your own.

DRUID STONES

Pay special attention to the beginning of this story where I seek to make the reader feel nervous and apprehensive, even though the PoV character is still confident and determined. I achieved this through the way I described the setting from the first sentence.

Throughout the story, I used several other methods to create vivid emotions. See if you can recognise them.

Barbed wire laced the top of the narrow gate, and the jagged end of a broken signpost stuck out of the gorse hedge. The owner of the land, it seemed, disliked people using the ancient Right of Way.

But whatever the farmer's quarrels with occasional tourists, modern-day druids or scholars of ancient history, it did not concern Kathy. She had come a long way to Cornwall on her first holiday since the divorce to explore the stone circles, and would not let a stretch of barbed wire stop her.

Unhooking the stiff latch, she allowed the gate to screech open. She squeezed through the gap, dodging thorny brambles and spider webs. She hated spiders, and no doubt many of them lurked in the dank growth. Hedges towered on either side of the overgrown trail, their branches heavy with water from the earlier rain.

Writing Vivid Emotions

On reaching the stile, she found it also seamed with barbed wire. There was no signpost, not even a broken one. The landowners seemed determined to block a public Right of Way. They might have trouble with vandals, litterers and crop-tramplers, but Kathy was none of these. She never interfered, never meddled, never left more than footprints. She had the right to see the remotest of the ancient monuments, the Dredhek Druid Stones.

Her jeans snagged as she climbed across the barbed stile. At fifty-five, she wasn't as agile as she'd been last time she'd visited stone circles. How long ago had that been? Almost forty years. She'd been on a youth holiday in Cornwall, dating a blond afro-haired boy from the campsite. Not that they'd seen many monuments. They'd been too absorbed necking under the hedgerows.

Whereas these days, Kathy would not miss the chance to experience the ancient magic. The earth energy surrounding Men-at-Tol and at the Merry Maidens had sent her dancing in honour of the elements. What would the Dredhek Druid Stones do to her?

On the other side of the stile, she found nothing but neck-high brambles, nettles, scratchy thistles. No path was in sight. The other stone circles had been easier to get to, even in the rain.

Should she retrace her steps? Perhaps she had taken a wrong turn somewhere, missing a stile or mistaking a plain gate for a kissing gate. The drizzle started again, and the printer's ink on the cheaply produced guidebook ran. Somewhere far away, a dog howled.

Step by step, she trudged across ploughed fields, treading down the thicket of bracken and thorny brambles. Soon, her trouser legs were soaked up to the knees and clods of clay soil clung to her trainers. When she sampled the first blackberries of the season, they tasted acid and gritty, with more pips than sour flesh. It couldn't be much further now, could it?

Suddenly the thicket cleared, as if by sorcery. Below her, twelve stones of grey granite stood chest-high, sticking from the sodden ground like teeth from scurvy gums. What a view! Excited, Kathy quickened her steps, impatient to touch the stones, all twelve of them.

As soon as she placed her hand on the rough surface of the nearest boulder, the ancient energy rose and tingled in her palm. The thirteenth stone, the one in the centre, beckoned strongest. Twice the height of the others, it stood tilted at a phallic angle. Its broad, flat back invited her to lean against it.

Below the overhang of the tilted stone, a posy of wildflowers wilted: yarrow, dandelion and gorse. How touching: someone still worshipped at this ancient site, where people had prayed for thousands of years.

She picked up the blooms. Beneath them lay the charred remains of a frog, its hind legs grotesquely sprawled.

She swallowed the welling sickness. So what if a group of neo-pagans or whatever they were wished to make a burnt offering? Thousands of animals got slaughtered everyday for food, and thousands of frogs got run over on the roads. They'd probably not burnt it alive anyway. Didn't Druids have the custom of triple deaths? They'd probably strangled it first and drained its blood before putting it on the fire. She had no business judging their customs.

As she replaced the flowers to hide the corpse, she recalled a glimpse of a druid ritual during that Cornish holiday decades ago. The memory descended like a damp cloud.

Roaming the fields in search of a private spot, she and Jerry had stumbled across a group of cloaked, hooded figures with sickles and staffs.

The druids, though polite, had made it clear they did not like outsiders watching their ritual. Kathy wanted to leave immediately, but Jerry walked right into the gathering to a pale, red-cloaked woman.

With his bell-bottom trousers and purple striped shirt, Jerry looked pathetic among the robed druids. "Are you all right, lady?" he asked. "Do you need help?"

"Ngnggggg." The woman swayed, staggered, and raised her arms. "Ongengeeee."

"The lady is our queen." The tallest of the druids pointed at her crown of wildflowers and ivy. "She's had a little too much fly agaric, but we're looking after her."

"Engeeeengeeee." The woman's diluted pupils confirmed that she was drugged.

Kathy pulled Jerry's sleeve. "Let's go. This is a private celebration, and they can do what they like. Freedom of religion and all that."

"That's right. Freedom of religion." The tall druid smiled benevolently and drew a sign in the air, not unlike the Christian blessing of the cross.

Still Jerry didn't budge. "She looks sick. She needs help."

"For God's sake, Jerry!" Kathy dragged him away. "This isn't your business. You're embarrassing me."

On their way back to the camp, they argued. Jerry kept worrying about the drugged woman, and Kathy kept telling him the druids knew what they were doing and he had no right to meddle. At last, he fell silent. But there had been no more kissing that night, and after that, their romance had fizzled out.

The memory of that long-ago quarrel, combined with the charred frog, spoilt the magical mood. Dusk was falling anyway: time to leave. A well-trodden path led westward across a ploughed field, probably to a remote country road. Perhaps that was the way she should have come, instead of scrambling across barbed wire fences.

A distant sound alerted her, a chanting like the hum of a coming swarm of bees mingled with the low beat of drums. Six figures approached with large strides, each carrying a staff, their white hooded robes flowing. Bronze sickles gleamed at their waists.

Unwilling to get caught up in another druid ritual, Kathy ducked between a hawthorn hedge and a pile of firewood part-covered with a green tarpaulin, to let them pass. Her trousers grew sodden and her legs cold. All around her thick, sticky spider threads hung with raindrops like glass-bead necklaces.

But the procession halted before the stone circle. They rammed torches into the ground. Soon, the flames hissed in the damp air.

If she crawled out of the undergrowth now, it would look as if she had been spying on their ritual. To avoid the embarrassment, she would have to stay hidden until they were done.

A tall man with a circlet on his head chuckled. "I wonder what the Red Goddess will send us as an offering this year."

"Something small, I hope," a woman piped up. "A mouse or a rabbit. The sheep last year took ages to bleed out, and then it wouldn't burn."

"This time, I've brought enough wood for a big animal." The man pointed to the tarpaulin-covered pile.

He intoned an invocation of the Red Goddess, his voice deep and resonant like that of the solo baritone in Kathy's church choir.

Damp chills crawled up Kathy's calves and her thighs cramped. Rain trickled from a hawthorn bough into her collar and slid down her spine, but she held still. The ritual could not take much longer.

Now the druids strode in a clockwise circle, stepping across the part-exposed stones. Splashes of mud soiled their pristine white robes.

"Summer's gifts, summer's sacrifice...." Their chant, low and musical, had a hypnotic quality.

The inside of Kathy's wrist tickled. A fat spider with striped legs was crawling into her sleeve. She squealed.

At once, a druid strode to her hedge and pointed his staff at her like a spear. His young pimply face shaped into a grin. "See what I've found hiding in the haws."

Kathy's heart hammered in her chest. "I'm sorry, I...I didn't mean to... I don't want to disturb you or to interfere or anything..."

He pulled her up by the wrist and hauled her into the circle.

"Now, now," the druid with the circlet chided. "Let's treat our guest with courtesy." To Kathy, he said, "If you wish to be part of our ritual, you're welcome."

"But-" One of the females frowned up at him.

He silenced her with an impatient flick of his sickle. "I'm in charge here." His voice had a sharp edge. "It is through me the ancient blood flows, through me the gods speak. Never forget that."

"It's all right," Kathy said hastily. "I really don't want to bother you. I ought to go, anyway."

"You're welcome to stay," the chief druid said. "Very welcome indeed. We celebrate Lughnasad, the ancient festival of the first harvest. Have some wine."

He offered her an earthenware cup.

"If you're sure you don't mind me watching your celebration." She took the clay beaker from his manicured fingers and sipped. It tasted odd. Probably a home-brewed herbal concoction.

"Drink all of it," he instructed in the tone of a dentist telling a patient to rinse her mouth.

The brew was potent, almost instantly stirring a dizzy spin in her head. Gratefully, she accepted a chunk of bread, broken from a plaited loaf, still fragrant from baking.

The druid pointed the staff at her. "Denims are not appropriate for a high festival."

"Sorry. I didn't expect to attend a druid celebration. I'd better go. I don't want to ruin your festival with the wrong clothes."

"Stay. We'll loan you a robe."

With a flick of his arm, he commanded the older woman druid, who brought a bulky velvet garment the colour of blood, with a hole in the head and holes for the arms.

"Thanks, but I'd rather not." Kathy struggled against the growing unease. "You've been very kind, I don't belong here."

All six drew close around her, chanting in low murmurs. Kathy struggled in vain as he pinned her arm to her back while another forced the red robe over her head.

The chief druid ripped the tarpaulin off the pyre and poured the contents of a canister. Petrol stink spread. Then a match scraped. Flames shot up, cackled and hissed.

"Lughnasad is the time of the year when tradition demands a sacrifice to the Red Goddess, to ensure a fertile harvest for the annual cycle. Terrible things happen when people don't obey." The chief druid strode up to Kathy and bend to peer into her face. She could smell the mint on his breath. He pressed a wreath of ivy on her scalp. "You're very welcome to join our ritual."

Kathy fought to break free.

A needle-sharp pain stabbed into her cheek, and again.

The younger female druid clutched the big pendant on her chest. "My former grove only ever used flowers and fruit. A rabbit, I can understand. Even a sheep. But –"

"This is my grove." The chief druid tapped his staff on the rock beneath his feet. "I make the decisions. This is how our grove has sacrificed for millennia; this is how we shall continue."

The young druid with gangly limbs fidgeted with his hood. "Won't she be missed? There'll be people looking for her."

The chief held up his arms. "The gods speak through me. This creature is alone here. She is alone in life. She is the offering the gods desire. Do you dare disobey the gods?' "

Kathy's mouth was swelling with numbness, like at the dentists. Dizziness clouded her mind, and her willpower seeped away. Her body sagged against the leaning centre stone. The rock's ancient chill seeped into her bones.

The chief took the sickle and caressed its blade. It gleamed in the torchlight. "You won't feel much pain when I cut your wrists," he assured her, using the same tone as a dentist telling a patient it would hurt just a little. "You'll be pleasantly tired and whoozy. We'll drain your blood, and strangle you, and then before you expire, we'll put you on the pyre for burning. Have some more wine and poppy juice."

"Hey, those kids are watching!" The pimply druid pointed his staff at clump of gorse.

Kathy twisted in her captor's tight grip to see a pair of curly-haired teenagers in flaring jeans. Rescue had arrived.

"Help me," she tried to call, but the sounds squeezing from her swollen mouth came out as "Ngnggg. Ongengeee."

The chief druid's hands clasped her arms like iron grips. "The lady is our queen. She's had a little too much fly agaric, but we're looking after her."

"Engeeeengeeee," Kathy pleaded desperately, imploring them with her eyes.

But the girl was pulling the boy away. "Let's go. This is a private celebration, and they can do what they like." She sounded embarrassed. "Freedom of religion and all that."

"That's right. Freedom of religion," the chief druid said. She felt his breath on her neck and smelled his minty toothpaste again.

The boy, bless him, seemed to sense that something was wrong. "She looks sick. She needs help."

"For God's sake, Jerry!" Even as Kathy implored them with her eyes, the girl was leaving, pulling the boy after her. "This isn't your business. You're embarrassing me."

In numbed disbelief, Kathy watched them walk away. The curly-haired boy once glanced back over his shoulder, then they were gone.

DOUBLE RAINBOWS

In this story, only one character appears 'live', but he goes through a wide spectrum of emotions, including smugness, triumph, satisfaction, pride, confidence, doubt, surprise, suspicion, apprehension, worry, fear, terror, panic (not exactly in this order) and many more. You may want to make a complete list, and observe how I conveyed them. Watch especially how I used the character's thoughts, setting descriptions and visceral responses to escalate the frightening feelings from mild to extreme.

A big challenge in writing this tale was to manipulate the reader's emotions so the reader likes Gerard far less than Gerard likes himself, yet still feels with him.

Gerard hurried down the spiral staircase of Sibyl's lighthouse, his shoes clanking on the metal steps. The blue steel hands of his Rolex showed 8.13. The tide had turned two hours ago, and he did not want to get his new boots wet as he hiked home.

The steep chalk path from the promontory to the seabed was slippery with smudge from the night's rain. The sea surface glinted like a diamond-sprinkled sheet, and the air smelled of salty seaweed. In the distance, gulls cackled and squealed.

His chest brimmed with pride at how well he had handled the situation. Breaking to your girlfriend that you would marry someone else required a delicate touch, especially if she was pregnant. At first, she had hurled reprimands. Then she had demanded that he leave her home. But the high tide already submerged the way out, and she had to let him stay the night. After a lot of coaxing and consoling, her rants subsided to sobs. Gently, he pointed out that as an artist, she was above conventions like monogamy and marriage, and that single motherhood was all the rage. When he assured her she would remain the love of his life, and promised to continue his Friday night visits, she had stared at him in wide-eyed wonder. By morning, she had clung to him with surprising passion.

Sibyl had amazing curves, flaming hair and a temper to match, vivid imagination but little practical sense. She refused to sell the dilapidated lighthouse to one of the wealthy buyers queuing for 'converted character properties', insisting she loved living surrounded by sea. Isolated when the tide rose twice a day, with only her paintings for company, she lived for Gerard's weekly visits.

Driftwood, whelk eggs and cuttlefish bones littered the low-tide seabed, and bundles of dark bladderwrack lay entangled like scorched spaghetti. As he skirted around chunky boulders, the smell of fishy seaweed grew stronger, wavering between fresh and foul.

Rust-brown shingle and splinters of flint crunched under his fast steps. He had three miles to cover before the incoming tide wet his feet.

In the east, the sun was already painting the sky a brisk blue, but in the north, a curtain of silver-grey rain still veiled the view. A rainbow beyond the promontory framed the lighthouse in bright glory. He squinted. Was that a second rainbow emerging inside the large one? Even as he looked, the faint hues strengthened. Two rainbows, two women – the perfect omen for his fortunate future. Sibyl had probably spotted it already. He pictured her standing at the large window in her round room, paintbrush in hand, plotting to shape the vision into a painting.

But Gerard had no time to linger and watch the rainbows grow, because the tide waited for no man. Everything about nature – the sun, the rain, the rainbows, the tides – followed complex rhythms, regular but never the same. All was calculable – he patted the tide table in his jeans pocket - yet never quite as expected. Atmospheric pressure, moon phases and such all played a role. Stirred by wind and swelled by the rain, today's sea was already higher than normal.

Waves swished and slurped and rustled across the shingle. He took firm, even steps past black rocks, across broken shells and white crab corpses. Water ran in thin streams between sand and stones, down the almost unnoticeable slope towards the sea.

Soon he would have both: a rich wife and an unconventional mistress. A fair man, he would give both women the attention they deserved, but this required skilful planning. Erica could not be relied upon to show the same flexibility as Sibyl; she might even expect to have her husband to herself. He had to show tact and not spoil her illusions. A job involving absences from home would help, preferably no longer in her father's employ.

At 8.22, he reached the mainland shore where cliffs towered like steep castle walls. Thirteen feet above, sparse grasses grew in cracks, and gorse shrubs clung to precarious holds. Below that, nothing found a grip on the stark rock face, nothing survived the high tide.

He had another hour and a quarter to walk on the seabed to the end of the cliff that lined the shore. The wind rose, whipped up waves and sculpted them into mountain ridges. Puddles filled, and water streamed into rock pools. With the hem of his shirt, he wiped the thin coating of salt from his spectacles, and squinted at the sea. The tide was coming faster than it should.

An illusion, no doubt, from a water level raised by wind and rain. Today's high tide was at 13.01, which meant the sea did not hit the cliff until 10.30, and then he would be past the inaccessible part and on dry secure land.

He checked his watch again, just in case. The blue steel hands on the silvered dial showed 8.28 as it should. A quick glance back revealed the bill already washed by water, the route he had walked submerged by the incoming tide. Only its tip, the rock with the lighthouse, still pointed like an admonishing finger out of the sea. The rainbow was now clearly a double, its colours sharp.

Ignoring natural laws, the water crawled closer, brushing the scattered rocks with angry lashes and frothy caress. Puddles filled and forced Gerard to take big strides from rock to rock.

He checked the tide table, ran his finger down the column for today's high tide. 13.01. He was right, and had an hour and a half to clear the rest of the cliff.

Was the sun supposed to stand so high at half past eight? All he knew was that it rose from the east. On previous walks, he had not paid it much attention. He always left Sibyl's place at low tide, which was a different time every week, so the sun was never in the same place anyway. Though the sun looked high, and the water was close.

What if his watch had stopped? A Swiss Rolex was supposed to be infallible. *Ticke-tac, ticke-tac, ticke-tac,* the watch assured him, and the minute hand moved another notch.

As the water's edge sneaked nearer, he scanned the cliff face for an escape. Surely there was some gap, some path, some stairs hewn into the rock? But he had walked this route on many Saturday mornings, and knew there was none. Thoughts and fears whirled through his mind, questions, worries and doubts.

A drop of sweat slid down his back, and another. Keeping close to the cliff, he marched faster.

Wall-like waves crashed and shoved sheets of white foam at his feet. Tendrils of panic curled into his stomach while gulls glided past in mocking calm.

A cloud blocked out the sun. The air chilled and pimpled the skin on his arms, even as the sweat of fear pasted the shirt to his back. To his left, the cliff stood smooth, steep, merciless.

Salty splashes stained his shoes, sneaked into his socks, soaked his trouser legs. The drum of fear beat in his chest. With the watch pressed to his ear, he ran.

Boom boom boom, his heart thudded. The watch went *ticke-tac, ticke-tac, ticke-tac* above the hiss of the waves.

The water rose fast. Icy wet snaked around his ankles, his calves. Still the cliff stretched without end.

No one could have reset the watch except last night. Suddenly he could explain how that happened.

Sweet Sybil. So grateful, so forgiving.

The next wave slammed his chest against the rock with ice-cold force.

DEAR READER,

I hope you found these tips helpful and will apply them to give your fiction the emotional power it deserves.

I'd love it if you could post a review on Amazon or some other book site where you have an account and posting privileges. Maybe you can mention what kind of fiction you write, and explain which chapters you found most helpful and why.

Email me the link to your review, and I'll send you a free review copy (ebook) of one of my other Writer's Craft books. Let me know which one you would like: *Writing Fight Scenes, Writing Scary Scenes, The Word-Loss Diet, Writing About Magic, Writing About Villains, Writing Dark Stories, Euphonics For Writers, Writing Short Stories to Promote Your Novels, Twitter for Writers, Why Does My Book Not Sell? 20 Simple Fixes, Writing Vivid Settings, How To Train Your Cat To Promote Your Book, Writing Deep Point of View, Getting Book Reviews, Novel Revision Prompt, Writing Vivid Dialogue, Writing Vivid Characters, Writing Book Blurbs and Synopses, Writing Vivid Plots, Write Your Way Out Of Depression: Practical Self-Therapy For Creative Writers.*

My email is *contact@raynehall.com*. Also drop me a line if you've spotted any typos which have escaped the proofreader's eagle eyes, or want to give me private feedback or have questions.

You can also contact me on Twitter: *https://twitter.com/RayneHall*. Tweet me that you've read this book, and I'll probably follow you back.

If you find this book helpful, it would be great if you could spread the word about it. Maybe you know other writers who would benefit.

I'm also adding an excerpt from another Writer's Craft Guide you may find useful: *Writing Deep Point of View*. I hope you like it.

With best wishes for your writing success,

Rayne Hall

ACKNOWLEDGEMENTS

I give sincere thanks to the beta readers and critiquers who read the draft chapters and offered valuable feedback: Margo Buzzard, Janet Wright, Yorgos KC, Philip T. Stephens, Douglas Kolacki, Larisa Walk, Daniela Smith, Amie Bjorklund, Usvaldo de Leon, Tammy Alexander, Katelyn Gehringer, Allie Dresser, Donna M Day, Joanne Wolff, Richela Rosales.

The book cover is by Erica Syverson and Uros Jovanovic. Julia Gibbs proofread the manuscript, and Bogdan Matei formatted the book.

And finally, I say thank you to my sweet black cat Sulu who snuggled on the desk between my arms with his paw on my wrist and his head in my elbow, purring his approval as I typed. No human expresses the feeling of content as eloquently as a cat.

Rayne Hall

EXCERPT: WRITING DEEP POINT OF VIEW

INTRODUCTION

Do you want to give the readers such a vivid experience that they feel the events of the story are real and they're right there? Do you want them to forget their own world and worries, and live in the main character's head and heart?

The magic wand for achieving this is Deep Point of View.

Deep Point of View is a recent development. Victorian authors didn't know its power. They wrote stories from a god-like perspective, knowing everything, seeing into everyone's mind and soul. 20th century writers discovered that when they let the reader into just one person's head, stories became more exciting and real.

If we take this one step further, and delve so deeply into one person's mind that the reader's awareness merges with that character's, we have Deep Point of View.

Readers love it, because it gives them the thrill of becoming a different person. The reader doesn't just read a story about a gladiator in the arena, an heiress in a Scottish castle, an explorer in the jungle, a courtesan in Renaissance Venice—she becomes that gladiator, heiress, explorer, courtesan.

Deep Point of View hooks readers from the start. After perusing the sample, he'll click 'buy now' because he simply must read on, and when he's reached the last page, he's grown addicted to the character, doesn't want the story to end, and buys the next book in the series at once.

A reader who has been in the grip of Deep Point of View may find other books dull and shallow. Who wants to read about a pirate, when you can be a pirate yourself? Immersed in Deep PoV, the reader enjoys the full thrills of the adventure from the safety of her armchair.

In this book, I'll reveal the powerful techniques employed by bestselling authors, and I'll show you how to apply them to rivet your readers. I'll start with the basics of Point of View—if you're already familiar with the concept, you can treat them as a refresher—and then guide you to advanced strategies for taking your reader deep.

This is not a beginners' book. It assumes that you have mastered the basics of the writer's craft and know how to create compelling fictional characters. If you like, you can use this book as a self-study class, approaching each chapter as a lesson and completing the assignments at the end of each session.

To avoid clunky constructions like 'he or she did this to him or her' I use sometimes 'he' and sometimes 'she'. With the exception of Chapter 6, everything I write applies to either gender. I use British English, so my grammar, punctuation, spellings and word choices may differ from what you're used to in American.

Now let's explore how you can lead your readers deep into your story.

Rayne Hall

CHAPTER 1: FRESH PERSPECTIVES

Instead of explaining Point of View, I'll let you experience it. Let's do a quick practical exercise.

Wherever you are right now, look out of the window (or step out into the open, or do whatever comes closest). If possible, open the window and stick your head out. What do you notice?

Return to your desk or notebook, and jot down two sentences about your spontaneous observations.

You can jot down anything—the cars rushing by, the rain-heavy clouds drawing up on the horizon, the scent of lilacs, the wasps

Writing Vivid Emotions

buzzing around the dumpster, the aeroplane scratching the sky, the empty beer cans in the gutter, the rain-glistening road, whatever. Don't bother writing beautiful prose—only the content matters. And only two sentences.

When you've done this—but not before—read on.

*

*

*

Have you written two sentences about what you observed outside the window? Good. Now we'll have fun.

Imagine that you're a different person. Pick one of these:

1. A 19-year-old female student, art major, currently planning to create a series of paintings of townscapes, keenly aware of colours and shapes.

2. A professional musician with sharp ears and a keen sense of rhythm.

3. An eighty-year-old man with painful arthritic knees which get worse in cold weather. He's visiting his daughter and disapproves of the place where she's living these days.

4. A retired health and safety inspector.

5. An architect whose hobby is local history.

6. A hobby gardener with a keen sense of smell.

7. A security consultant assessing the place where a foreign royal princess is going to walk among the people next week.

Once again, stick your head out of the window. What do you notice this time? Return to your desk and jot down two sentences.

I bet the observations are very different! Each time, you saw, heard and smelled the same place—but the first time you experienced it as yourself (from your Point of View) and the second time, as a fictional character (from that character's PoV).

You may want to repeat this exercise with another character from the list, to deepen your insight and practise the skill. If you're an eager learner, do all seven. This will give you a powerful understanding of how PoV works.

Now let's take it one step further: Imagine you're the main character from the story you're currently writing (or have recently finished). How would he experience this place? What would he notice above all else? Again, write two sentences.

Now you've experienced the power of PoV, this is how you will write all your fiction.

ASSIGNMENT

Repeat this exercise in a different place—perhaps when you have time to kill during a train journey or in the dentist's waiting room.